Atomic Time

Elissa Rashkin

Nixes Mate Books
Allston, Massachusetts

Copyright © 2019 Elissa Rashkin

Book design by d'Entremont
Cover photograph from the collection of Lauren Leja

All rights reserved. This book or any portion thereof may not be reproduced or used in any manner whatsoever without the express written permission of the publisher except for the use of brief quotations in a book review or scholarly journal.

ISBN 978-1-949279-08-5

Nixes Mate Books
POBox 1179
Allston, MA 02134
nixesmate.pub/books

To Ian of Pas de Chance, for never letting go

Contents

Ghosts	1
The Chosen People	3
Judenrat	4
Kaddish	8
If I Were to Have One Last Wish…	10
Flame	12
Sometimes Even the Flowers	14
Eulogy: A Year w/o Love	15
Civilization and Its Discontents	20
Cantina	22
Middle Passage	24
Caliban	26
Huntress	29
Work Song	30
Atomic Time	32
Glass	34
The Wait	36

Airport	38
California	40
Wreckages	42
No One Told Us There Would Be Fish in the Sea	44
Currents	45
Land	46
A Sudden Gust of Wind	47
Godard at 85	48
Rolling Sideways	50
Requiem	51
Bloodlines	53
Angels	56
Against Demons	59
On the Killing of Women	60
There Is Blood	62
Kaddish for Chantal	66

Atomic Time

Ghosts

We come not to praise but to torture

The world's ghosts
arise
again
where we thought
there had been transcendence.

    Ayotzinapa
    Ferguson
    Gaza
    a thousand cities
    burning…

Paint turns
to blood as it splashes
the board
coagulation
burnt fingers
fractured limbs
(cannot
look
away)

A white veil
floats
under the eaves
a thin voice
shivers…

I pluck
my eyes
from the canvas
trying
trying
trying

All I have left
this fading vision

The Chosen People

They say the grandfather
used to spit on the ground
each day when he passed
the synagogue.
Reluctant fruit
of the rabbinical tree.

Hatred makes no fine distinctions.
A Jew is a Jew and the devil will have his due:
G-d closed his eyes
the army came
and tossed the bodies
into a common grave.
One brother crawled out, broke
in pieces, to tell the story.
The family fled to Romania. The black waters
failed to recede. I wake up

each night

barely breathing

in my broken brother's body
trying
to claw our way out

Judenrat

What torture this
to choose between fatalities
and the lives of others.
If I hand over the strong
at the black ghetto gate
the rest will remain
to fight to the death
for crumbs fallen
from an ill-gotten
basket of bread.
If I surrender the child
w/her scarce nine springtimes,
the firstborn
is safe,
this lugubrious
day neverending.
Or if, like Abraham,
I sacrifice the newly born
so that youth may harbor
the dubious hope
of reproducing.
Or if I tear the crust
from the grandmother's lips

o live
y.
a knife in my chest
h grim
ɔn, leaving

, in the end,
n flock?)

heroism
tes open
e scatters –
: those
claim the reward
hide,

p the children.
ter the train

ai is with us still
ıo bayonets nor ovens

no indifference
just behind that distant mountain
must be Jerusalem.

The lout that stuck a dagger
in my wife's ribcage
tasted one time or another
the flavor of the word
"brother,"
together we celebrated
a child's first breath;
my son, handed over
to the soldiers
at the ghetto's entrance
at the exit to never ever more.

And no one parts the sea in two
and no one causes manna to fall
to lessen the hunger
nor water
to these mouths
agonizing
with thirst.

In the forest there are no trees
only the hunter.
I
Judenrat
I
incarnation
G–d's betrayal
The name
we never utter
because it contains light
because it contains darkness.

Kaddish

I, poet, convoke this minyan of infidels
to mourn and to celebrate
what remains of our humanity.

Kaddish for the disappeared
Kaddish for the headless, dismembered
limbs in black plastic garbage bags;
Kaddish for the meth-crazed warriors
broken lovers, dead neglected children
Kaddish for the junkies
for the suicides (lord have mercy), may
their pain dissipate
across clear skies
of lovingkindness.

Kaddish for the rest of us
left to wonder
to pretend
or to defend
against numberless hosts
to raise our sons and daughters
from their hidden graves

To raise our sons and daughters
to rise, and rise again
to exorcise the demons
to sing
so fiercely
until there is nothing
left
of song.

If I Were to Have One Last Wish...

If I were to have one last wish it would be silence

Like Prometheus who was told
in no uncertain terms
not to play with fire

And then they came and ripped out his entrails
and then they came and tore you out of my womb
and then they came and threw us into the fire
and then they came and never stopped coming after

And my womb it is still bleeding
though every night
I rewind the fabric
mend the intestines
wipe away the blood
like the scarf of Penelope

If I were to have one last wish it would be silence
an end to this scream
an end to the dream
that comes with the pills
and exhaustion

and the vultures
that tear you from my womb each night
as if otherwise
I were to forget
the fire
that perhaps I only
brushed
without
intention
a mortal confusion
that ends in the isolation ward
of this great cellblock
called
consciousness
where thousands of jailers comply
with the rules, fill out the forms,
stamp the papers
signed by an indifferent god
who denies
one last wish

Flame

I call upon the faith of my ancestors:
This drop of oil must last for days
and the temple shall be redeemed.

She
who dissolves
she
who hungers no longer
she
who waits
gazing
into the flame

To remember
the desert
and the open sea
the boats of refuge
prosperity
the gray streets,
sleet, wool-
wrapped
wanderers
in a city

of damp concrete
of diffuse
light

I call upon the faith
this drop of oil
this temple gate
this resurrection
in time and space
this flame unbent
before
the violent wind

Sometimes Even the Flowers

Sometimes even the flowers
are bullets, this rain
flooding land-mined streets
all the way home
under murderous skies.
The war years

were just like this, unspeakable
desires staining the hands
of each passer-by.
Even the oak trees connive
and betray, their twisted
roots stabbing the sidewalk
canted angles broken limbs
the unnatural gait of the earth,
a borderless vertigo
that propels you toward the sea:
yr only scale model
of eternity.

Eulogy: A Year w/o Love

do you think i never dreamed this
dream before? no i
peeled and raw and
glistening i approached
something resembling
a name
something looking a lot like
a kind of a feeling that some-
one might have recognized
"i wanted so much"
i had so much
once
to give.
i could have
died so many seconds
foaming at the mouth
gunshot whisper
a spark, never
igniting
the dried needles
carpet of memory. do
you think i never
dreamed this dream before?

womb collapsing into
packages of brittle
empty membrane, the mucus
corazón, called
something by another name
in a language
inadmissible of vigilance.

the surgery accomplished i
put a record on the turntable
and weave slowly
a waltz sans rhythm
a color uglier, deeper
than the depth
called blue.
do you think i never dreamed
of tender seas, misspent
waves of rage
disguised as hope
as spontaneous amputation
as windburnt folly?

did you think it was you,
this howl of acquiescence?
your hand slicing skin

nervous reluctant manipulation
did you think i was not brave?
certainly
i was not brave.
split scatter of seeds
dark universe waiting
to be born.

hand reach-
ing towards my heart
meeting only entrails
tongue bite
bile and rancor.
no one forgives
such decay. i had hoped
to come by it
honestly, a name
that would name
what cannot be claimed.
but one year/one moment
makes me a thief,
for this:

cut my fingers
swell my veins until

they transmit oceans.
float on yr very own life-
raft, toss kisses
into every harbor.
for this is the year
that no one drowns
explicitly
that no one is forced
to confess, that no
one steps out of line,
the lining
that keeps
you from slipping
from bridges of your own
pathetic need. do you think
i never dreamed this dream
before?
the truth is i have
never slept
and do not sleep
and will not sleep
the pulse of the living,
a red wet muscle
a corpse whose eyes do
not close, no matter

how much the living
avoid its gaze

do you think i have
not broken
ribs, overturned birdcages
in a last ditch attempt
at flying free?

there is
a name for this and it is not
white light
it is not sadness
it is not anything
that rolls off anyone's lips
late at night in the coils
of a telephone cord
in yesterday's postmark
in dreams that have not been recorded
that have not been dreamed
that anyone
remembers

Civilization and Its Discontents
(A rehearsal for corpses)

syphilitic swoon on the floorboards
gnaw raw ankle
bone open

there is a picnic
but it takes place in a slaughterhouse

she: "there were
roses once
then
nothing"

she: a dry death
behind yr eyes
you drank the poison
now yr shit glitters

syphilization and its dis/contents

he: needle sticks in her thighs
i wouldve thought

await abscess
abyss

myself: hey! that thumping bassline
is not yr heart!

gnaw raw arteries
mucus seeping
sarcophagus valentine
like you guessed

in each other/skeletal
would be romantic
w/o so many ants

yes we will call this a picnic
complete with champagne,
wet-naps, demerol, and
tv. let us not
forget the local anesthetic
and human sacrifice.
cordon off the dead mans zone.
red velvet to hide the stain.

Cantina

this hand-me-down cantina
everyone here is refugee
some know it
while others aspire to significance,
squeezing discolored memories
from a digital jukebox

refugee duo plays for coin:
choose a tune
from a wrinkled repertoire,
boozy lament, w/accordion
& country guitar
(hrs later they go, wallets full
and the rest are empty
because reading & writing
are suddenly not enough)

refugee waitperson juggles tabs
and 1 poet thinks how she really
should get going before the streets
are empty and bleak

outside is no-woman's-land
and the refugees keep on dancing
the refugee waltz

yet another weekend
in a broken little city
reeking of murder
rain and apocalypse

Middle Passage

Everyone knows that stars are dead
their light a ghostly afterglow

But then we forget
that oceans are full of shipwreck
waves / remains
bones become foam
shackles that rust like pirate gold
coral for bones

Thousands of messages
set adrift in shattered bottles
telegrams lost in the spiral
frequencies of wayward
galaxies

The steamy air of port towns
heavy with farewell
and those footsteps
that never arrived

First the piers, rotting fish disintegrating nets
then the raucous square, spilled sugar marimba

where captives are sold at auction
whips and blood / forgotten like starlight
walls encrusted with coral

Forgotten like starlight
gleaming like starlight;
look up in the sky
at the ghosts of the Middle Passage…

Caliban

> *You taught me language; and my profit on't*
> *Is, I know how to curse. The red plague rid you*
> *For learning me your language!*
> — Shakespeare, *The Tempest*

Fuck you America
and I do mean both continents:
torture slavery prostitution
cadavers blackmail strange fruit.
Hunger and its thousand ghosts.
Fuck you Mister President
Lear jet limousine million dollar hairdo
and the multitudes
ain't got no shoes
ain't got no vocal cords
ain't singing no blues
under the ground

And no one knows
if the DNA match
matches yr child
or some other collateral
damage

narcoestado
AK-47
survival of the fittest
or the chickens
coming home
to roost.

Little children for sale
drooling suicide in progress

Fuck you cops with yr wrong directions
fuck you dynamite blasted mountainside
dried up rivers bald forest the last jaguar
shot down
digital surveillance
not a word;
fuck you temple w/ yr demented blessings
fuck you newspaper of promises and lies
fuck you free television
cable television
streaming video
cellular decay
perhaps you don't remember

I did not invite you
to my island

Shackles and chains
is all I know
at the wrong end of a gun
you taught me yr language
and my profit on it
is this:
I know
how to curse
and one more thing too,
taught to me
in the silence
of resistance:

the master's tools
will never dismantle
the master's house[1]

---

[1] Audre Lorde, "The Master's Tools Will Never Dismantle the Master's House," in *Sister Outsider*, Freedom, CA: Crossing Press, 1984.

Huntress

I'm not a woman who knows Latin,
but I do sometimes
speak in tongues.
My shoulders are sea-cliffs,
jungles grow along
the amazon of my thighs.
I carry knives
inside my veins.
A woman born of women,
thick stone wombs
smelling of placenta and incense.
Soft knots of hair
wise and soothing breasts
shawls that spill harvests.
Always a daughter,
I spin around the sun
the earth's tilt never
takes me by surprise.
In the sky dark animals wander,
my entourage:
their feet the color of thunder
their pointed eyes,
stars.

Work Song

scraped red my
inside
liver tongue
wet
shoes slip
a glossolalia of petals

the sun is going
the utter absence
banana trees no
water falls
just the opening and shut
no i don't want
to pull my head from
this viscous fabric

there is hope and then
there is no hope
there is no hope and then
there is hope

appear
a ticket or a sign
something
to move this thing
keep me
breathe
deeply
smells of other dimensions

unrequited lust for g–d

Atomic Time

biting yr lip you
hit the floor running
and the noise behind you
didn't diminish
the relentless tango of
forward. oh you
stand in one place.

so you laid in his bed all
radiant as hell, spitfire
glowworm in heat, quivering
insect limbs.
you sucked his cock and
only later
remembered the factory
where rows of women paint
clock faces with liquid uranium
licking the tips of brushes
to keep their fine points.
it's not the plague
so much as the risk of losing
yourself forever.
but everything is a crapshoot

with crooked dice, your
earrings broken your
jacket torn. so when
he comes in your mouth you
swallow, millions of little deaths
kicking and contorting
yr way back to life

Glass

smash the windshield of ego
superfluous chrome
stretch wrought of velocity
eyeline matches of lust
and smothered disaster

not chastity
not charity
demons in mirrors
closer than they appear

> a machete
> swallows
> tunnels
> of memory
> of whisper
> of longing

strap torn from the ceiling
limp and useless in your hand
limp and useless as your hand
which trembles as you
shake away the shards

for a few seconds you wonder
and then the blood
returns you to the surface
of an earth as unscathed
as your clearcut forearm
as your snowcovered thigh
as your volcanic womb

not chastity: you want
to devour everything on
god's green planet
to jumpstart your
affirmation of life.
this wedding is a potlatch.
the bride split open on the dinner
table, on the altar, on the
hood of a steaming machine.
blood tongues
outline lacy breast
collision sacrifice
obsidian and glass

grasses lick crimson and sandy
remnants, foreboding
siren of approaching ambulance:

your animal howl

The Wait

a hundred year's wake
a rotten carcass, movie
of your life.
if you see it in a dream,
it'll happen. if your
nails peel back, eyes shrink
your tongue roughens.
belly swells, feet implode.

if you forget –
you are lost.
when the phone rings,
it's always long distance.
time crawls backwards.

there are snails creeping
in yr ears. yr hair is wet w/mucus.
(if you listen hard,
you can almost hear the telephone.)

if the world were flat
you'd seize it and ride
glide across waves of centuries

of mass hysteria, of prayer wail
of bitter herb, of pantomime
and glass and amber
of insect juices
of predatory innocence
of water
of water
of water
be there in no time
no time at all

Airport

that nun over there
looking for a place to plug in
& check her electronic bible –
and me, I have nothing to declare:
where I've come from, what
was I doing, how long
I don't know the answers
to these questions, nor why
we are in line at starbucks,
or what is in all the big
suitcases

where these people get
so many words

my head throbs w/disaster
we have finally arrived
we must be entering
celebration mode
but of this I would never
post a selfie;

maybe a little scribble
on the bathroom wall
EJR was here/
then gone

California

Same-old knotted hills
dry grasses ablaze
riverbeds empty of expectation
somebody's heroin overdose
another pretend suicide.

You would think there would be healing
you would think and have it wrong;
one more Sunday shooting, no rain,
mess of cut-up arms.

The ocean is an unwinnable argument
nor is it my business
to know who's name's changed
whose illness is now irrefutable
whose body just plain
drifted out to sea
who are all these sunglass-strangers
walking the same chihuahua

At the end of the day
California is just a word
for get me out of here
an imperceptible decay
everything on fire
an ancient, frozen horizon
the waves/the waves/the waves

Wreckages

Counter-wise conjecture:
is it correct to call the self a *wreck* or
is it *wretch*, smashing thru lenses like
rice paper windows, gulping random
mouthfuls, eyes red w/
expectation.

Oh fire
oh fire, oh rage
and the red sky
over Disneyland

Today there are
tidal waves under
the earth, someone lost,
nothing found; bricks
shatter, boulders tumble
from rooftops and
balconies, is the air
ever going to clear
out there…

Watching / waiting
raging / wrecking /
kneeling /
retching / then
merely
abiding –

Everywhere you look
something is
falling; I say,
someone
should be caterwauling
right about now
over the glacier
w/amazing grace

No One Told Us There Would Be Fish in the Sea

Whatever information
we had at the beginning
was clearly wrong.
It's not a jungle out there. In fact,
the streets are full of bears
forgetting the forest on little screens.
Look at me, I'm limping! Grrr,
go the bears.
Something is not right, I kept
thinking, and then the next person
who came along was the blind man,
knocking canes.

No one takes care of us when we're sick.
The frying pan stays empty
no matter how long we stare
at that mocking black mirror.
It was supposed to be a joke, but
fell flat. *No one told us
there would be fish in the sea!*
Except there aren't any, any longer,
except in cans. You just keep
swimming. Watch out for nets.

Currents

Someday I will declare this landscape complete
stretched as it is with folded paper,
pebbles, read and
unread books, tides low
and steady w/the movement
of small currents.
Bed of rock
fragments of colored glass
polished soft by the uneven
breath of dreams

Someday water will spill out
the edges, rivulets seeking
level ground, only to disappear
in patches of coarse sand.
Shells, ground to sparkling powder
become the dust
of a curative elixir
where the spirits lay deep
under the debris
& the waves turn over
to worship the moon

Land

you my ashy sierra
my desert
my tundra.

lower drawbridge
let me in. fortress
yr eyes.
yr open throat.

moon swallowing demon

you my eclipse
my apocalypse

my forest
of a thousand fractured
meteors.

you the tierra
that rushes towards my feet
then slips
atomic/glassine/quicksand
never actually
landing

A Sudden Gust of Wind

glittered afternoon
shudder of birds
ocean wail. simmering
celestial oven.
the sand is white
as ice cream, voluptuous
and sticky,
caressing the backs
of towels, undersides
of fallen trees.
rut of sage and juniper.
i am soaked to my ankles, then
a sudden gust of wind makes me
sputter and whirl

except that there is
no wind today
only a tug on a kitestring
some capricious mercury
dragging me back towards the sun
and you:

icarus naked

Godard at 85

once upon a time, life
was a series of perfect shots.

the city stinks of piss,
is a battleground.
under the marquee we dodge bullets
till the torches dim and flicker
and clowns burst through the paper screen
swallowing grenades and juggling machine guns
but nobody's laughing.
o nostalgia.
popcorn spills to the floor and remains, an eternity.

JEAN-PAUL BELMONDO
throws a match to the floor
rubs a thumb across his mouth
and smiles
because he is about to die
and at the same time,
to live forever

jump cut
it's a thousand years later
marx actually did drown in coca-cola
and spielberg's counting his billions
whether we watch his movies or not
because microchips in our brain
make movie theaters obsolete

but godard, oh godard
throwing luminous darts from yr dark cave

"go toward the light
and shine it on our night"

by *cinema* we meant you

Rolling Sideways

the plaza just before the rain
freezes like Pompeii.
a child's hand sticks to her accordion
a woman about to unfurl a black umbrella.
pickpocket's fingers forever stretched
towards the tourist's purse.
something drops from the balcony,
where the president, inside, is sleeping
off the crisis.
just before the rain
the cathedral and all its saints
roll sideways,
imperceptible,
pasted precariously on an earth
that trembles like the ocean.

who was it who took
that blurred picture
who wrote that shiver of a song
the one strummed by the barefoot man
on the corner of independence
and apocalypse
on an ancient guitar
with worn frets
and no strings

Requiem

poison oak tangles
roots unravel
mud soaked dust.
ant, wasp, any
thing that crawls
beyond the judgment
of judgment.
strangers aimless
dry wilderness.
the center of the earth
is here, in your
discomfort, your
dis/ease. call it
the downfall of corpo-
rate erotica.

devices are useless here.
jokes get you nowhere.
yr gun smacks the bark
of indifferent trees, or
echoes through deep canyons.
if you desire to live,
suck on acorns and dry grass;

learn to fly. circular
like vultures.
learn to sting,
to howl.

nothing will be built here.
fistfuls of lizards emerge from
swollen tombs.
there is nothing that is not profane.
if there is an elegy
it is only the wind.

Bloodlines

Arrive before dawn. Line up. Take a number.

There is not
enough blood
to fill the arteries
of the sick and wounded.

Our arms are pale
not enough blood
to fill
the emptiness
to revive the dead
to sustain
the wheel of life
spiraling
its slow and sudden
gyrations.

There are not enough medics
to receive
the offering.
Come back tomorrow. Line up.
Line up, maybe tomorrow

you can take a number.

(In the tower lay the dying)

Our veins
in danger of collapse
our blood poisoned
I do not desire
the solidarity of
extermination
the slow death
bureaucratic
not dramatic

Entrails
arteries
a number
wait in line
soon it will all be over.

In the tower lay the dying.
In the streets there are machine guns.
In the streams and mountains,
fields and vacant lots,
common graves.

The hospital is a morgue.
Take a number.
Add them up.
Reclaim your corpse
on the way out
wash your hands
sign out before leaving.

Angels

dead
in a pool
of mystery
no photos
we are
a transitional
people
you knew
no place
for us just
this
and
jail
w/out a dime
to call home
so did you signal
with weed
stolen postage
with the ink
tattooed down
yr neck

(3 kids play

in a basement
a father sleeps
night shift growl
japanese/american
los angeles
samurai angels
and all
the unwritten
letters)

did they forget
to tell you it was
knives
outside
panther
eyes
give us away
jump cut
and nowhere
to hide
did they tell you
about america
how it was

not a play
ground
or did they just
forget, such
a tangential
history, a
post-it or footnote
to the main event
whatever that is
we the makeshift
we the chosen
we the blessed
we the dead

Against Demons

oh lord, i've
tangled up the sheets again,
awakened sweating
from the misbehavior of sleep.
my dreams are seaweed, free
falls, dystopic disneylands built of
membranes and upside-down memories.
i would like to stay up all night,
to stare down the empty bed,
its pillow eyelids. the tentacles
of exhaustion enfold and overwhelm
their sorry prey. caught
between soft stickiness like
the pearl in the oyster. like venus
in her fly trap.

if i die before
i wake, let me break
clean of dreaming, let me stake
my soul and play all my aces
in short, deliver me
free of ghosts, blood and spiders
a cool hand on my forehead
parched bones
wrapped in swaddling

On the Killing of Women

the cops knew. they always do.
a broken condom. two
steak knives taped together.
some cat hairs
in the back of a van.
the phone was off the hook. unplugged.
the cord was cut.
a plastic shoe found in the alley.
the police knew. they always do.

100,000 peasants equals one diplomat.
haiti and all of africa
together make paris. three
bosnias is oklahoma city.
all the dead women in the world
don't add up to john wayne bobbit's
severed dick.

you have the right, no, the obligation
to remain silent.
a twenty dollar whore
has no value in the equation. zero
plus zero equals zero.

anything you say, do, wear, use or imagine
can & will be held against you.
yr rapist will grin
as he drives your body to the morgue.

There is Blood

There is blood
surging from unsuspected
fissures that I hesitate
to call *wounds*

The wound is INSIDE

You are an anonymous
human, let's say:
mechanic, male, age 25
or seller of junk metal
student of metaphysics
somebody's unemployed child
inexplicably chopped into pieces and
stuffed in a plastic bag
left to rot on heaven's doorstep

Sometimes my womb
still bleeds
the children
are left
to navigate
the abyss

and the mothers
wring our hands and weep
(I weep for thee and thine
I weep, oh lord, I weep)

Yet, they are wounds!
I dissipate:
there is strange blood
in my hair or
on the tablecloth
in books and slips of paper
we bleed
bleed for thee
my love, anonymous
my child
of woman born

Give me yr hand, child
let them not
take you away
let them not
fire at random
steal soul

let them not
judge what is innocent
let them not
bereave
lord let them not
throw you away
in a garbage bag
lord oh lord
have mercy

...and if I could
connect
the bones
reconnect tissue
please speak to me
yr battered mouth
(oh child o my child)

this is not a lament
there is no funeral urn
there are no
roses
these are roses
these words
I give unto you

petals
a bed of petals
a blood of petals
a ribbon of thorns
a river of mourning
a crescendo, a cry
a blessing, a goodbye
glossolalia
hunger and thirst
weeping
adios

Kaddish for Chantal

Art begets art
as sorrow begets sorrow

If there had been no Godard
If we had never sat in darkness
suddenly dazzled
by luminous oceans
and the thin air
of motionless
contemplation

If Karina and Belmondo
had never set foot
on that imagined island
if Jean-Paul's thumb had never
swept across
his lips
to brush away the dust of cinema
to build anew

If there had been no Auschwitz
no six million flames extinguished;
what other memories would our blood carry
like hidden poison

If the mother's tasks had been undertaken
in utter silence
without the camera's caress
would we understand love
without its absence

If each object
reproduced itself in miniature to enter the eye
if there were no camera obscura
if a woman had never dared
to gaze upon another
retaining the imprint on the retina
her gestures
not forced
to look away
if we had never received this gift
of light and shadow
Chantal

Sorrow begets sorrow
the kitchen, the bed, the screen
the tenderness of orphans
the making and unmaking of graven images
then the last unmaking
turns out to be sacrosanct

Acknowledgments

Thanks to the editors of the following publications where some of these poems originally appeared.

Kaddish : *Former People: Bangs, Whimpers, Art, Culture, and Commentary*
Atomic Time : *Quinceañera*, Pas de Chance Press
Kaddish for Chantal : *Nixes Mate Review*
The Chosen People : *Nixes Mate Review*

Thanks also to the editors, my friends, colleagues, and family, especially my parents, La Red Independiente de Mujeres Escritoras, and Ariel. To my girls Laura Lizbeth, Anna, and Xochikiauitl: *gracias por la inspiración*.

About the Author

Elissa Rashkin is a writer, historian, and professor of cultural and communication studies at the Universidad Veracruzana, Mexico. Her books include *The Stridentist Movement in Mexico: The Avant-Garde and Cultural Change in the 1920s* and *Women Filmmakers in Mexico: The Country of Which We Dream.*

42° 19' 47.9" N   70° 56' 43.9" W

Nixes Mate is a navigational hazard in Boston Harbor used during the colonial period to gibbet and hang pirates and mutineers.

Nixes Mate Books features small-batch artisanal literature, created by writers who use all 26 letters of the alphabet and then some, honing their craft the time-honored way: one line at a time.

nixesmate.pub/books